THE LUNAR CYCLE
Phases of the Moon

Genevieve O'Mara

The Rosen Publishing Group's
PowerKids Press™

New York

Published in 2009 by The Rosen Publishing Group, Inc.
29 East 21st Street, New York, NY 10010

Book Design: Daniel Hosek

Photo Credits: Cover, pp. 3, 4, 6, 8, 9 (moon), 10, 11 (moon), 12, 14, 16, 18, 19 (moon), 20, 22 (moon),
23, 24 © Nando Machado/Shutterstock; p. 5 © William Attard McCarthy/Shutterstock; pp. 9 (Earth), 11 (Earth),
15 (Earth), 21 (solar eclipse), 22 (astronaut) © Photodisc; p. 7 © Thomas Nord/Shutterstock; p. 13 ©
dabobabo/Shutterstock; p. 15 (moons) © Tamara Kulikova/Shutterstock; p. 17 © Osvaldru/Shutterstock;
p. 19 (Earth) © NASA/Getty Images; p. 21 (lunar eclipse) © Diego Barucco/Shutterstock.

Library of Congress Cataloging-in-Publication Data

O'Mara, Genevieve.
  The lunar cycle : phases of the moon / Genevieve O'Mara.
    p. cm. -- (Real life readers)
  Includes index.
  ISBN: 978-1-4358-0002-1
  6-pack ISBN: 978-1-4358-0004-5
  ISBN 978-1-4358-2973-2 (hardcover)
  1. Moon--Phases--Juvenile literature. 2. Moon--Juvenile literature. I. Title.
  QB588.O53 2009
  523.3'2--dc22
                              2008036789

Manufactured in the United States of America

Contents

Earth's Moon

On a clear night, the biggest and brightest object in the sky is the moon. The moon is made of rocks and **minerals**. It doesn't make its own light the way the sun does. The moon's light comes from the sun. The sun's rays **reflect** off the moon's surface and make it look as if the moon is glowing.

The moon looks large because it's closer to Earth than the stars or other space objects. The moon is actually much smaller than Earth. In fact, some scientists think that the moon was originally part of Earth! They think that a large object crashed into Earth long ago and broke off a piece that became the moon.

Although Earth has only one moon, some planets have several moons.

5

Layers of air surround Earth and keep it from getting too hot or too cold. The moon has no air around it. It gets very hot in sunlight and very cold without sunlight.

Even without special tools, we can see the moon's light and dark spots. These spots show us that the moon's surface isn't smooth. It has flat plains, tall mountains, and narrow valleys. Long ago, hot liquid rock, or lava, flowed out of the moon. It cooled and formed these features.

The moon has craters, too. Giant space rocks hitting the moon's surface caused many of these holes. The biggest crater is over 700 miles (1,126 km) wide!

Without air, there's no wind or weather on the moon. Nothing can grow there.

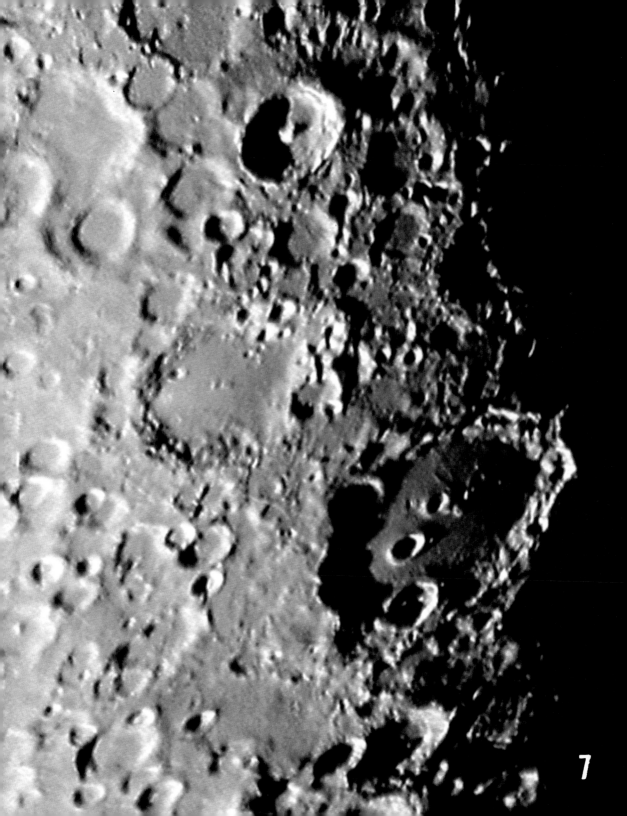

7

The Moon's Path

Because of Earth's **gravity**, the moon **orbits** Earth instead of flying into space. It orbits Earth every 27 days and 8 hours. It moves from west to east as it orbits Earth. However, it looks as if it moves from east to west. This is because the moon orbits Earth much more slowly than Earth spins.

The moon is always the same shape, but we often see only part of the lighted side. It looks different each night because it's in a different spot in its trip around Earth. Changes in how the moon appears are called **phases**.

The moon's oval path sometimes brings it closer to Earth. This makes the moon look larger.

Phases of the Moon

A cycle is a chain of events that happen in the same over and over again. Can you think of some cycles? Plant growth is a cycle. A plant starts from a seed, grows, makes more seeds, and dies. The new seeds start the cycle again. phases of the moon are a cycle, too. They happen in the s: order over and over again.

A **lunar** phase called the new moon happens when tl moon moves between the sun and Earth. The side of the moon facing the sun is lit. The side of the moon facing Ea is dark. The moon may be dimly lit by earthshine, which sunlight reflected off Earth.

We may see a ring of sunlight around the moon during the new-moon phase.

11

On the night after a new moon, we see a small part of the moon's east edge. Each night, more of the moon can be seen. The moon waxes, or seems to grow larger, each night.

About 7 days after a new moon, we can see half of the moon's circle shape. This phase is called the first quarter because the moon has completed one-quarter of its path.

About 7 days after the first quarter, the moon has moved until we can see its full shape. This is a full moon. It happens when Earth is between the moon and the sun. The sun lights the entire side of the moon facing Earth.

Since the lunar cycle repeats about every 28 days, there may be more than one full moon in a month.

After the full-moon phase, less of the moon can be seen each night. When the moon seems to grow smaller, we say it wanes.

Around 7 days after the full moon, about one-half of the moon is lit. The bright half is the side opposite the side that's lighted in the first-quarter moon. This phase is called the last, or third, quarter. At this time, the moon has completed three-quarters of the lunar cycle.

Seven days after the last quarter, the moon enters the new-moon phase again. Once more, we can't see the moon since it's between the sun and Earth. The lunar cycle starts again.

When the moon looks smaller than half of a full moon, it's called crescent. When the moon looks larger than half of a full moon but smaller than a full moon, it's called gibbous.

LUNAR PHASES

First Quarter

Waxing Crescent

Waxing Gibbous

S U N L I G H T

Full

New

Waning Gibbous

Waning Crescent

Third Quarter

Another Lunar Cycle

Did you ever notice that the moon appears in the sky each day at different times? The moon rises and sets in a cycle, too.

Like the sun, the moon seems to rise in the east and set in the west. Around the new-moon phase, it rises at almost the same time the sun does. It also moves across the sky close behind the sun. The moon starts to rise about 50 minutes later each day. It travels farther behind the sun each day, too. By the full-moon phase, it doesn't rise until the sun sets.

During each lunar cycle, you may be able to see the moon in the sky during the day.

The Moon and Tides

The moon has gravity that pulls on Earth. Its gravity causes tides in large bodies of water, such as oceans. The side of Earth facing the moon has a high tide. The moon's gravity also causes a high tide on the opposite side of Earth. The areas between have low tides. The moon's force of gravity is weakest in these places.

The Earth turns, so the moon's gravity pulls on different areas during the day. This makes the tides change. High tides happen about every 12 hours and 25 minutes.

Every large body of water has two high tides and two low tides each day.

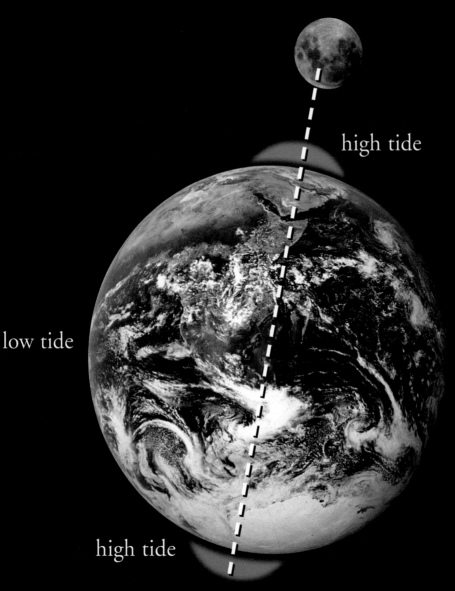

high tide

low tide

low tide

high tide

| **CAUSE** the moon's gravity pulls on Earth | **EFFECT** high tide at the parts of Earth nearest and farthest from moon |
| | **EFFECT** low tide at the parts of Earth between the high tides |

19

Eclipses

Two or three times a year, Earth's shadow passes over a full moon. This is called a lunar **eclipse**. Earth's shadow blocks the sunlight that normally lights the full moon.

The moon causes another kind of eclipse. Twice a year, the sun, the moon, and Earth are lined up during a new moon so that the moon makes a shadow on Earth. This is called a solar eclipse. Depending on where you are, the moon may block the sun completely or only **partially**.

You can watch a lunar eclipse safely. However, because of the sun's bright rays, solar eclipses are dangerous to watch without special tools.

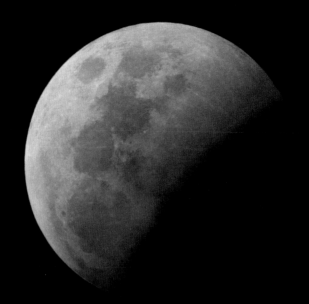

partial lunar eclipse

solar eclipse

Learning About the Moon

Thousands of years ago, people believed the moon had magic power. However, people also knew that the lunar cycle could be used to measure time. The word "month" actually comes from a word that means "moon."

We've learned much from **astronauts** who have been to the moon and studied it. But there are still mysteries to explain. Some matter in moon soil is found nowhere on Earth. Scientists hope to study this matter and the moon more in the future.

Astronauts Neil Armstrong and Edwin "Buzz" Aldrin landed on the moon in 1969.

Glossary

astronaut (AS-truh-nawt) Someone trained to travel in space and explore it.

eclipse (ih-KLIHPS) When one space object partly or completely hides another space object.

gravity (GRA-vuh-tee) The force that pulls things toward Earth or the moon.

layer (LAY-uhr) A thickness of something that lies over or under something else.

lunar (LOO-nuhr) Having to do with the moon.

mineral (MIHN-ruhl) Something found in soil that is not a plant, animal, or other living thing.

orbit (OHR-buht) To move around an object in space because of the force of gravity.

partially (PAHR-shuh-lee) In a manner that affects a part but not the whole.

phase (FAYZ) A step or stage in a number of events that happen over and over.

reflect (rih-FLEHKT) To hit something and come back.

Index

Due to the changing nature of Internet links, The Rosen Publishing Group, Inc., has developed an online list of Web sites related to the subject of this book. This site is updated regularly. Please use this link to access the list: http://www.rcbmlinks.com/rlr/lunar